VIKING
FREELANCING

Viking Freelancing Page

Chapter 1:

Intro to Freelancing

At first glance, freelancing can seem like a dream come true. Choosing your own hours, working on something new every other week, not having to leave your couch- what job could be better? Freelancing can be an exciting, rewarding and uniquely flexible career choice, but like any job, it has its downsides. Knowing how the industry works before quitting your job and jumping in to full-time freelancing is essential; that's where this book comes in.

Freelancing is an incredibly exciting endeavour and as a relatively new area in the world of work, it can be difficult to inform yourself on how it all works. But don't worry, once you've read this book you'll be ready to embrace the world of freelancing and make money on your terms.

Freelancers are self-employed workers who are hired by clients to provide specific services, usually on a short-term contract basis. The biggest difference between working as a freelancer and a full-time employee is flexibility. As a freelancer, you decide who you work for, what projects you accept, where you work, and what your schedule will be like. Freelancing is a viable career option for anyone with a computer, internet connection, and space to work. If you're a self-starter who likes to control your daily work, then freelancing could be the perfect choice for you!

When working as a full-time employee for a company, you answer to someone above you and work according to deadlines and goals set by them. This relationship changes with freelancing. While your client is paying you, they aren't your boss. A client often won't know how long it will take you to complete the work they're asking of you; it's up to you to set a deadline you know works for you. Your client will have goals for you, but these goals will be much more negotiable than those set in a traditional employer/employee setting.

The following are the most popular areas in which to become a freelancer, and some of the jobs within those areas:

Programming

This section can be broken down into two categories: software and web development. With all programming jobs, finding your niche is a good way to build up a portfolio. If you're particularly strong in one programming language or at creating specific products, focus on that. This will help you to build a name as a specialist and allow you to improve one skill to a very high level rather than being just another freelancer who does a bit of everything.

Writing

Content writing (e.g. blogs, articles), copywriting (e.g. product descriptions, website page content), and technical writing (e.g. user manuals, reports) are the most popular styles of writing for which freelancers are hired. A lot of freelance writers write similar pieces for the same clients on a regular basis; for example, writing a monthly article for an online publication.

Graphic Design

As a lot of companies use freelancers for marketing and advertising work, the majority of freelance graphic design work involves designing advertisements and websites. When working as a freelance designer, it's important to learn how clients communicate visual ideas using words; otherwise, you could spend a lot of time on unsatisfactory first drafts.

Administration

Virtual assistants have grown very popular in recent years, as much of an assistant's work is now done online or over the phone. Administration jobs such as social media and website managers are also very popular. These freelancers are experts on a company's products and answer any questions that consumers post on their online media, as well as posting regular content such as blog posts.

Video Editing

As video sites like YouTube and Vimeo have soared in popularity, almost all social media platforms have added a video element in order to capitalise on this success. If you're interested in becoming a freelance video editor, this is great news! Freelance video editing will feature a lot more work on small-scale projects than in-house work, so don't expect to be working on big-budget films or TV shows any time soon.

Marketing

Social media management and copywriting also fall into this category, but of course, there are a wide variety of freelance marketing jobs. Marketing has changed dramatically in the last few years, from outbound (the company reaching out to the consumer) to inbound (the consumer reaching out to the company). This means that a lot of marketing work now focuses on making information on a product available so a consumer can access it when they're researching a potential purchase.

Chapter 2:
Where to find Work

While some freelancers use a blog or email newsletter to find clients, there are dozens of freelance platforms that help beginners to find work. A freelance platform is a marketplace where freelancers and clients both have profiles.

Clients post jobs that they want completed, and freelancers respond with their interest. When you speak with a client, you tell them why you can do this job well and the client can view your profile (which is discussed more in Chapter Three), examine your portfolio, and see reviews from other clients.

Many of these platforms use escrow, meaning that the client's money is saved by the site when your contract begins and released to you when the work is completed. This can provide great security when working with unknown clients. Below are breakdowns of five of the biggest and most popular freelance platforms.

Upwork

Upwork is one of the most popular freelance platforms around and has over 1.5 million users, including every job type that freelancers are used for. Upwork is free to join, but takes 20% of the money you make. Upwork allows you to set your experience level and choose between being paid by the hour or per project. If you choose to be paid per project, each contract can be broken down into milestones so you can still be paid regularly.

PeoplePerHour

PeoplePerHour is mostly aimed at web projects, but all positions can be advertised. This site is more popular for programmers than other freelancers. Freelancers must pay to use PeoplePerHour if they want to send more than 15 proposals to clients per month, which means there are a smaller number of users. PeoplePerHour also takes 20% of any money you earn.

Guru

Freelancers can see how much a client has spent through Guru before working with them to see if they are viable and how much they can expect to earn. Guru has a daily job-matching feature to let you know about jobs that might suit you, as well as a work room to help you manage your projects. Guru takes 8.95% of your fee if you have a free account, and 4.95% if you pay a monthly subscription charge of $39.95.

Toptal

Toptal does not cater to all freelance areas; it exclusively provides web developers, designers, and finance experts. Toptal is also exclusive when it comes to the freelancers themselves; the site employs an extensive screening process and only accepts those with a high level of experience. It boasts that it only accepts 3% of the freelancers that apply to the site. This high level of member means that rates on Toptal are higher than other sites.

Freelancer

As well as hourly and long-term contracts similar to other sites, Freelancer offers "contests", where a client posts a job with a money prize, and freelancers bid on the project with their submissions. Freelancer takes 10% of the money you earn.

Chapter 3:
Getting Clients

Once you've found the right freelance platform for you, you need to do two things: create a high-quality profile, and secure clients.

Creating a Profile

A freelance profile allows potential clients to learn about you and view your portfolio in one place. Think of it as a more detailed version of a CV and cover letter. Your profile will be formatted in different ways depending on which platform you use, but the two key elements are a description of your skills and a strong portfolio.

Most freelance platforms will have beginner guides that help you to create a solid profile. While these are a great place to start, make sure to add something extra that's unique to you. Check out the top freelancers' profiles on the site you're using, then compare them to less successful profiles; what are the differences? A lot of the time, it's personality. As a freelancer, you're marketing yourself, so don't be afraid to show who you are. List your experience, your work preferences, and what you hope to get out of being a freelancer. Feel free to add a short description of yourself and include a bit of humour. Clients hiring freelancers want someone they can communicate with, so adding a personal touch will make you seem more approachable and easy to work with.

Depending on your profession, your portfolio might be varied or specific. For example, a graphic designer's portfolio might include website layouts, logos and print content, but a software developer's portfolio might only feature Python projects. What you include in your portfolio shows clients what you're interested in working on; don't include examples of work if you don't intend to do that work again. If you want varied projects, include varied work; if you want to focus on a niche area, only include samples of that area.

A common mistake for beginners is to include a sample from every project they've ever done. While this does show you've done a lot, a prospective client won't want to scroll through a long list to find something relevant to their project. Choose a dozen or so of your best pieces from the last two years; don't include content older than this unless it is exceptional. As you secure work, change out some of these older pieces if you create something better. You can build up your portfolio as your freelance career grows, but it's best to start small.

Securing Clients

It's that age-old adage; you need experience to get a job, and a job to get experience. Most clients look for experienced freelancers who they feel they can trust to complete the project, so it can be difficult to secure your first few jobs and build a name for yourself. The best way to do this is to charge a low amount. Unless you have some money saved, don't quit your day job as soon as you begin freelancing. With a low rate, you will be able to secure those first few jobs and get positive reviews on your profile. It will probably take a few months to build up enough work so you can charge a rate you're happy with. Once you're doing enough work at a high enough rate that you can support yourself, you can move into full-time freelancing.

Freelancing can be financially unstable, as how much money you make completely depends on the amount of work you do from week to week. The best way to stabilise your income is to build relationships with a select number of clients and work with them as often as possible. Writers might produce monthly content for a website, or marketing analysts might work with a company every quarter. Whatever area you work in, identifying sources of recurring work is the key to a steady income.

Conclusion

After reading this book, you should know what freelancing is, what kind of freelancer you can become, and how to do it. If not, go back and start again!

Freelancing is a uniquely rewarding career path, but you need to have initiative and determination in order to succeed at it. Find your niche, choose your marketplace, and build your brand. It might not be as glamorous as you dreamed, but starting small will help you to grow your freelance career into something amazing.

Working as a freelancer means you're your own boss. This has the obvious perks of creating your own schedule and choosing what you work on, but it also means that you need to be strict with yourself. Re-evaluate your profile every so often, update your portfolio, and examine the direction of your career. It's a bit of extra work, but definitely worth it.

www.ingramcontent.com/pod-product-compliance
Lightning Source LLC
Chambersburg PA
CBHW071446210326
41597CB00020B/3952